# A Guide to

# System

# Design

# Interviews

Expert Tips for Acing System Design Interview Questions without Stress

# CARL

# JONES

# Copyright

# Table of Contents

# CHAPTER ONE

## GETTING IT RIGHT FROM THE ONSET: ACING YOUR INTERVIEW

Just like a conventional interview for a business or management role, system design interview also requires you to follow the basic etiquettes of attending an interview to get the job. Don't forget that your first impression matters more. Dress well, wear nice cologne, speak well and don't feel intimidated are the basic tips you must have come across in interview books. Of course, these tips are necessary to boost your overall performance and make you stand out from most other candidates eyeing the job. But as you improve your appearance, you should also improve the level of reasoning you are bringing along with you on the interview day.

A system design interview, unlike most conventional interviews, entails you to design a working system that will handle core tasks for an organization. Have you ever attended an interview where you were asked to design a chat system that will allow every worker in the organization chat conveniently and share files with each other during holidays? That is one clue into system design interviews. This is an interview that allows you to showcase your skills.

Although, system design interview might seem complex and tedious at first (when you hear it), as you will wonder why would anyone ask you to, in a space of 30 minutes, design a particular product – say X – that has taken computer scientists and engineering gurus some X years to build? It is not possible right? Not if you read this guide. Look – for instance – at what happens when you Google search; the simplicity and how everything seems effortless like the developers didn't even put in effort at all. But behind the scene, the amount of technical know-how and the level of sophisticated technologies behind what you see is something you can only imagine.

Now that you have gotten an interview invite for that System Design job that you applied for, it is in your best interest to give it your best and come out successfully and that is where this guide has been written at this crucial time to give you a shot of what the interviewers want from you – which they are not willing to, in any way, let you know. Let us turn the table a little bit and imagine yourself at the other end of the divide where you are the CEO or one of the hiring coordinators interviewing a candidate for a system design role in your organization. To a reasonable extent, your eye will be on that candidate that was able to impress you the most with his gift of gab through answering all the questions you asked correctly. This is how you put yourself in the shoe of the interviewer and see for yourself what you would most probably be looking for in a candidate while interviewing for a role like this.

The first wrong impression most candidates have about interviews is that their interview skills and dressing will very much get them the job. While this might be true – to a small degree and in few cases – it is not always advisable to always bank on these two skills only. Interviewers are also looking out for other qualities such as; ability to work under pressure, ability to collaborate effectively under minimal supervision, ability to communicate effectively amidst some other skills pertaining to personalities. At the same time, there are few red flags most computer experts, engineers and designers are not aware of, and they even think is perhaps a sought after quality. Over – engineering is a big problem most engineers are not even aware of, as they believe in designing only pure systems while not minding the cost. Companies are looking for a way to maximize profits and minimize expenditure. If there is a way companies can produce valuable products using some less expensive alternatives, they would most probably shift to that direction. Come across as someone who understands this and is willing to help the company drive fortune while still minding consumers' satisfaction and products' usability.

This chapter will talk about some tips to help you ace your next System Design interview

1. **Practice makes perfection**

This is probably the most clichéd expression you have been coming across since your high school days. You have probably heard your Mathematics telling you the same thing as he gives you complex algebra or trigonometry to battle with. Yes, your teacher was right. Practice makes perfection. You will always have an edge in anything you take time to figure out. The best footballer doesn't just practice for a day and stop there hoping to become the best. He takes his time practicing countless times before he becomes a professional at what he does. The same scenario is applicable here. You will need to prepare ahead of the interview day if you are planning to wow your interviewers and get the job. There are many ways you can practice ahead for your next interview, but this guide will talk about a peer-to-peer mock interview session where you have your close friend or an online mock interview system. The mock interview system is typically an unstructured interview system where you will be able to assess your performance against some set standards that will be measured in the real life interview system. Essentially, the mock interview session will help you hone your skills under a very conducive environment using real interview questions. The following tips can help you when you want to set up a mock interview session between you and your friend or any online interview platform;

- **Inform your friend prior to the time so he/she can be aware of what you want to do:** Tell your friend how you want the interview session to be, what question they can ask you and the standards you are expecting them to measure. If you don't know what interview questions to practice with, be on the lookout for some real life interview scenario later in this book.

- **Set up a collaborative and conducive environment:** Interviews are not just done in anyhow condition. You must set up a good environment by replicating what is likely to be obtainable on the interview day. Invite your friend over at your place and get started with the interview. You must also try and eliminate distraction as much as possible. At the moment, there is a wave of Covid19 Pandemic and you can possibly set up a video session over Zoom or any other teleconferencing app.

- **Provide feedback:** Have your friend provide you with the feedback of the interview. He/she should let you know about the areas that you need to work on. The feedback should be sincere and not biased or flawed with destructive criticism.
- **Keep practicing:** You can have about two more sessions before the final interview day.

## 2. What exactly does the interviewers want from you

While system design interview has, nowadays, become a critical part of the core process for recruiting system designers into an organization; it is okay to tell that System design interview will not necessarily request you to write lines of codes that can be compiled or run off hands. You will most likely be faced with questions asking you to design a functioning large scale distribution system like YouTube, a chat based platform like WhatsApp, a URL shortening system and other open ended questions. During your interview, you should endeavor to – as much as possible – let your line of communication be open ended at all times while providing answers to the questions. Your performance in a System Design Interview (SDI) is usually assessed on these criteria;

- **Your Knowledge base:** This cannot be said enough. The knowledge that you have in your head will always open doors while answering these open ended questions. You must know how to synchronize what you have learnt in theory and apply them to solve real life problems.

- **The way you tell your ideas in a way that is sufficient enough to drive home your point:** No other means of assessing your knowledge than to see if you can really teach and explain it to the interviewers. Assemble your ideas together and correlate them in a simple and convincing manner that shows you actually know what you are talking about. Lead the conversation and tell the interviewers why "A will work" and "B will not." Discussing the advantage and disadvantage of each design method will; let the interviewer see you as someone who will really put in great effort on the job.

- **Discuss about the operational efficiency:** When you are faced with a System design question, you will need to tackle it with achievable steps and talk about the relevant interfaces involved in the system design. Some practices you can familiarize yourself with include;
  - o **Operational requirements:** Define the end goal of the system you are designing and clarify any ambiguity before getting started. This will allow you to understand the exact scope of the design at hand
  - o **Define your system interfaces:** Understand and define expected APIs for the system.
  - o **System Scale Estimation:** Make sure that you comprehend the scope of the system at hand
  - o **Defining Data Models:** Provide clarity as to how data will flow between the different components of your system.

This allows better partitioning and management of data.

- o **Go from simple to complex:** Understand those components that will be required to solve the System Design question you are given, first on a simple level, and then take it up a notch.

- o **Understand how to mitigate side effects:** Check and verify if there is any error if an error is likely to come up later in the process, and then figure out ways to mitigate them.

- **Your ability to be able to improve the system should there be any need to do so:** There is no perfect system, and while this is not a statement to embrace mediocrity, it is important to convince your interviewers that you can always improve the system, if there is any need to do so in the future. This will not only gain you points but also tell them that you believe in the system and you are always willing to improve on anything.

- **Bring your critical thinking skills along:** System design needs people that can think critically and get their way around complex situations in no time. One way you can demonstrate this is to sketch designs on the board as you tackle questions while brainstorming with the interviewers. Keep a note and jot down important observations and points.

- **Ability to understand the question asked:** One common mistake candidates do is not asking questions or get more clarity on the questions interviewers asked them. Interviewers are human beings like you and there is no offense if you ask them for clarity on the questions they asked you. This will show you are confident and you are not cowed by their appearance. The only thing is that you should ensure you asked quality questions. Refrain from asking questions about their personal lives, love affairs, beliefs, religion, families or how much they earn. Asking interviewers questions not directly in line with the purpose of the interview will be seen as a turn off and you should avoid this as much as possible.

- **Networking, abstraction, database, reliability availability etc.** are also skills that you can showcase to the interviewers to stand a chance. Another very important thing you should understand is never to lie about your ability to do a thing that you cannot really do. Most candidates lie about their abilities during an interview just to get the job. This will not always go unnoticed as one or two questions about your abilities will always send you off track and you will come off as not being trustworthy or desperate. Be genuine as much as possible while you work on yourself to be good at some important skills before the interview day.

Having understood what the interviewers are hoping to see in you, let us try and take a critical look of how you can apply the interview tips above to solve design interview problems. The steps below provide flesh and will enable grasp the practical approach to attempting and acing all design problems.

- **Understand the design problem at hand and establish the scope of the design**

While giving a headshot at what you should be while trying to understand the question being asked, it is important to show you what you should not be. This will get you on the right track to being the kind of person interviewers are hoping to meet on the D-day. Look at the analysis below;

In a class of about 60 students, David has always been the first to answer any question thrown to the class by their teacher. He takes joy in being able to answer all the questions fast even before the teacher finished asking. Whether David knows the answer or not, he will always raise his hands to answer questions. Of course, David will be the cynosure of the class and will be liked by the teacher because he is responsive and fast. While attempting a System Design Interview, if there is anything or anyone you should not be, it is David.

In a System Design Interview, giving out answers as if you know what is in the interviewers' head is not a good thing. You don't give answers before the interviewer finishes talking. This is to allow you take your time, ponder about the question being asked and then provide the right answer. You will only be able to do this if you don't jump at the question before the interviewer says the last thing.

As a scientist or an engineer, you were probably taught how to tackle hard problems and dive into the final design when you were in college; but this approach – if followed – will prompt you to design a wrong system for a simple task. One skill you should bring along, as it has been discussed previously, is your ability to ask questions in case of ambiguity, make right assumptions and arm yourself with every detail needed to build the right system for a specific task. In this regard, you should be willing to ask questions as and when due.

When you ask for clarity during an interview, the interviewer either tries to answer your question straight or tells you to use your assumptions. If you are asked to use your assumption, clearly put down all assumptions that come into your brain on a piece of paper or whiteboard as you will always need them at a later time.

The kind of questions you can ask are the ones that seek to further understand the requirement. You can consider the list of questions below to guide you;

- What specific functions or additions are you expected to build with the system?
- How many end users will this product have?
- What are the future projections of the company? What are the plans that the company has in place to scale up on their systems?
- Is there any design or services that the company had done in the past which you can leverage and improve on? What is the technology stack of the company?

# Typical Examples

Let us say, a particular company X is interviewing you and you have been asked to design a workable news feed system or platform. The following conversation can ensue between you and the interviewer to seek for clarity about what you have been asked to do;

**You**: Is this web app, a mobile app or can be deployed on both web and mobile?
**Interviewer**: It is both a mobile and a web system.

**You**: What important features must this product incorporate?
**Interviewer**: The user must be able to make a post and see active news feed as they are being shared.

**You**: Should the news feed be sorted in a reverse chronological order or there is a particular order in which they have to be sorted? In fact, you can even proceed to ask for more clarity at this point. Ask if they want posts from the admin or some organizers to be more important than random posts from anyone (admin posts will always be placed at the top of other posts).
**Interviewer**: Let the feeds be sorted in reverse chronological order.

**You**: On this system or app, how many friends can one user have?
**Interviewer**: 9000

**You**: Can I know the expected daily, weekly, monthly or yearly traffic volume for this system or app?
**Interviewer**: 500000 daily active users (DAU)

**You**: Can the users share videos or images?
**Interviewer**:  The feed should contain media files, like video and images.

The above are likely questions or chats that you can ask the interviewers. These questions will clear all doubts and arm you with the necessary details.

## Propose high-level design and reach an agreement with your interviewers

This involves developing a high-grade design and then reaches a conclusion with your interviewer on the design. Collaboration with your interviewer is a great start toward building a successful product.

- Design an initial template of the whole design. Ask the interviewers what they think about the blueprint. Engage your interviewers and let them be involved in your success. Many interviewers are happy when they are carried along and are involved in the design step.

- Map out key components using a paper or the whiteboard. This can feature things like APIs, data stores, cache, message que, CDN, clients (mobile/web).
- Carry out a back-of-the-envelope calculation to check if the blueprint will fit the scale constraints. Tell you result to the interviewers and let them provide you with feedback.

If you can, kindly go through some solid use cases. This will let you frame your high-level design. It is also very possible that the use cases will guide toward discovering edge cases that you have not even considered.

*Example*

Let us deploy "Design a news feed system" to show how to approach the high-level design.

At the high level, the design is partitioned into two flows: feed publishing and news feed building.

- Feed publishing: when any user (be it admin or anyone) publishes a post, the corresponding data will be written into cache/database, and that post will be populated into friends' news feed.
- Newsfeed building: the news feed is built by aggregating friends' posts in a reverse chronological order.

## Design deep dive

Already, you and your interviewer should have reac-hed a reasonable milestone and must have marked the following objectives;

- An agreement on the system's overall goals and feature scope
- Mapped out a high-level blueprint for your overall design
- Gotten sincere feedback from the interviewer on your high-level design
- Had some ground ideas about where to focus on in deep dive based on the interviewer's feedback

You should try and work with your interviewer to identify and prioritize components in the architecture. It is worth telling that every interview is different. Sometimes, your interviewers might give you hints that they like you to focus on high-level design. Sometimes, if you are in for a senior candidate interview, the whole discussion could be on the system performance characteristics, bordering on the bottlenecks and resource estimations. In most other cases, your interviewer may tell you to go into details of some system components. For URL shortener, it is exhilarating to go into the hash function design that changes a long URL to a short one. For a chat system, how to reduce latency and ways you can support online/offline status are two sound and hot topics.

Ability to manage your time effectively during the interview is key, as it is especially very easy to get carried away with some small and irrelevant details that don't necessarily show your detailed abilities. Try not to dabble into unnecessary details and repetitions.

## Wrap up

In the last stage of the interview, the interviewer might allow you to talk about some additional points or ask you some follow up questions to further assess your abilities. You can consider the key directions below;

- Just like you have been made to understand that no system is perfect, your interviewer might want to know the bottlenecks in your design and few improvements that can be done in the future to further improve your system's usability. The key thing here is not to tell the interviewers that your work is perfect and it needs no modification or improvement going forward. There will always be one or two things that can be improved in the system. This is, in fact, another way of displaying your A − game and leaves a fine impression that lasts.
- You can also consider giving your interviewer a brief recap of your system design. Let this be short as much as possible and should be like an overall summary of everything you have done. If

you had previously talked about some solutions to some problems, this is another chance to add and build upon it. Refreshing the interviewer's brain is a good one after your session.

- Talk about some error cases, such as network failure, server failure etc.
- Talk about a few operation issues. How will you monitor metrics and some error logs that might occur during the system's deployment? How will users start the system?
- Discuss how significant things you have added in your system design can pave way for future upgrading. For instance, if you have designed an app where users can only have about 5000 followers, feel free to tell the interviewers whether there is a significant upgrade that can be done to the app in the future to allow users to have 10000 followers and even more.
- Talk about other refinements if there is time.

While wrapping up this session, the following are the recap of what you can do and what you should not do during SDI;

## Dos

- Don't always assume that you have understood everything asked. Feel free to ask for clarification if needs be. And do not always think that your assumption is the only correct assumption.

- Try as much as possible to comprehend the nature of the problem you are presented with.
- There is no one fits all solution anywhere. System design interviews are always open ended. This means that a solution that was designed by a particular designer X to solve a specific task Y in a startup company might be different from the one to solve the same problem in one of the big four. Ensure you take cognizance of the requirements and the end users.
- Let your interviewer know what is on your mind. Establish communication with your interview as soon as possible.
- Suggest more than one approach to one problem if you can.
- Talk about your blueprint with the panel, and once they agree proceed with the proper design.
- Let the interviewers be your partner in the journey. Engage them as often as possible.
- Do not give up on anything. Keep doing your best. Keep practicing.

# Don'ts

- Going to the interview unprepared is the first recipe to failure.
- Don't dabble into the solution without a proper clarity of what you are expected to do.
- Don't give everything too soon. Proceed from simple to complex.
- Ask your interviewers for help if needs be. They are not robots and they are expected to give you hints to keep you going.
- Talk. Effective communication between you and your interviewers can actually go a long way to augment your success rate. Don't imagine things in silence.
- There is always time to ask for feedback from your interviewers. Do not assume the interview session is over once you deliver the design. Do not stand up and make for the door if you have not been told to do so. Your interviewers are the ones in the right position to let you know when the session is over.

# CHAPTER TWO

## DESIGNING A CHAT SYSTEM LIKE WhatsApp

In this age and time, almost everyone is using one chat app or another. Some of the most popular chat apps include WhatsApp, Facebook Messenger, Telegram, Snapchat, Hangout, Skype, WeChat etc. These chat apps have become popular over time because of their simplicity (user experience is okay) and the fact that they are able to send chats, audio, videos and files within a reasonable space of time. To different people, chat apps represent different views and functions; and that is why you need to know the actual requirement for the chat app in question. What if the interviewer intends developing a chat app that only focuses on group chat and you went ahead to develop a chatting app that captures only one-on-one chat. This is why clarity is very important, just like it has been discussed in the previous chapter.

Now that you are in an interview environment or you are even in the process of preparing for one, designing a chat app is one System Design Interview problem you would like to familiarize yourself with.

## Step 1 - Understanding the problem and establishing your design scope

It is expedient to agree on the category of chat app the interviewer wants you to design. Nowadays, we have one-on-one chat apps like Facebook Messenger, WhatsApp, WeChat etc and office chat apps that concentrate more on group chat like Slack, or game chat apps, like Discord, that concentrate more on large group interaction with low voice chat latency.

Your first clarity question should border on what your interviewer wants you to develop by asking you to design a chat app. Ask the interviewer if it is a one-on-one chat app like WhatsApp or a group chat app. Some of the questions you can have in mind include;

**You:** What type of chat app do you want me to design? Is it a one-on-one chat app like WhatsApp or group based like Slack?
Interviewer: It should be a chat app for group chat and should also support a one-on-one chatting system.

**You:** Should it be a web app? Or a mobile app? Or both Web and Mobile apps?
Interviewer: It should be a Mobile app and a Web app. This means that it should have a web version and a mobile version.

**You:** What user capacity are you hoping to accommodate with this app?
Interviewer: It should support, without crashing, about 500,000 daily active users (DAU).

**You:** What should be the maximum limit for members in a group chat?

Interviewer: The group should be able to accommodate a maximum of 250 members.

**You:** What features should the chat app incorporate? Do you want the app to support files attachment?

**Interviewer:** One-on-One chat must be supported, group chat must be supported and also there must be an online indicator to show online presence (for instance, WhatsApp has a green that shows online users). The app will only support text messages for now.

**You:** Is there a limit to the message size? How long should characters be?

Interviewer: Yes, there will be a message size limit. The length of text should not be more than 100,000 characters long.

**You:** Should the chat, just like WhatsApp, be end-to-end encrypted.

**Interviewer:** Not necessary at the moment. However, there should be a chance for future app upgrades.

**You:** How long should the chat history be stored? Can the chat be deleted automatically for users after a specific period?

**Interviewer:** Forever. The chat can only be deleted by the users when they want.

In this section, let us focus on designing a chat app like WhatsApp that will focus on the features below;

- A one-on-one chat with unnoticeable delay between when the message is sent and when it is processed (low delivery latency). Note that high delivery latency will chase users away; much like sending a text today and it only got delivered after two days.
- A not so large group chat (say about 100 members).
- An online presence indicator.
- Can support multiple devices at a time. Users will be able to login to their account on multiple devices at a time.
- Supports Push notifications. This means the app will be able to send users automated messages even when they are not online.

It is equally pertinent that you agree on the app design scale. This app will support about 50 million daily active users (DAU).

## Step 2 – Talk about high-level design

While thinking about developing a high-quality design, a fundamental idea about how communication between clients and servers looks like is actually essential. While developing a chat system, you should understand that clients could either be web applications or a mobile application. There is no direct communication between clients, as communication is sent to a server first before it is delivered to the receiver. In order word, clients only communicate with a chat service that has the above mentioned features. The chat service you want to develop here must provide support for the functions below;

- Must be to receive messages from some other clients.
- Locate the right recipients for each message sent and deliver the message to the recipients.
- When the message recipient is not online, the chat service should be able to hold the messages for the recipient on the server until the recipient is online.

When a particular client (sender in this case) intends to initiate a chat, the chat service will be connected using one or more active network protocols. For a chat service, the choice of reliable network protocol is actually essential. You should talk about this with your interviewer.

For most server/client apps, requests are often initiated by the client. This is equally true from the sender's side in a chat app. When a message is sent from the sender to the receiver via the chat service, the HTTP protocol is deployed. The time tested HTTP protocol is the most common web protocol used by some of the most popular chat apps like Facebook messenger. Here, the client launches a HTTP connection with the chat service and forwards the message. This action will inform the chat service to forward the message to the receiver. Persistent connection between the sender and the chat service is maintained with the keep-alive header.

However, things are a bit more edgy at the receiver side. For one, HTTP is initiated by the client, it is not unimportant to send messages from the server. Nowadays, many techniques are in place to ensure a good server-initiated connection. These techniques include; **Polling, Long polling** and **WebSocket.** These techniques are essential and are mostly used during System Design Interview (SDI). A brief examination of each of these techniques can be found below;

## Polling

Clients can use polling periodically to ask the server if there is any available message to send. Depending on the rate/extent at which a client carries out polling, polling can be a little expensive. Imagine using your server resources to ask the server a question that comes out to be a No.

# Long polling

Due to the uncertainty in the Polling method, the long polling method seems to be a viable alternative.

In the long polling technique, a client will be able to still keep the connection open until new messages are actually available or a timeout limit has been reached. Once the client gets a new message, another request is sent immediately to the server and the whole process starts all over again. Although, long polling method avoids wastage of precious server resources, it still – nonetheless – has some limitations;

- Sender and receiver may be unable to connect to the same chat server. Servers based on HTTP are oftentimes stateless.
- A server has no perfect means to notify if a client has been disconnected.
- It is not really efficient. If a particular user does not chat really much, long polling will still be making periodic connections once timeout has been passed.

# WebSocket

WebSocket is the most common deployment that users can use to send asynchronous updates (updates sent after the first one has been completed and not at regular interval) from server to client. WebSocket connection is often started by the client. It is usually bi-directional and persistent. It begins its life as a HTTP connection and could –within reasonable time - be "upgraded" through some well-defined handshake to a WebSocket connection. Through this persistent connection, a server could send updates to a client.

It has been established earlier that the HTTP protocol is okay for use on the sender side. Nevertheless, you can also use it on the receiver side, as it is bi-directional.

The whole design process is simplified and design implementation becomes more straightforward when you use WebSocket for sending and receiving messages. Since WebSocket connections are often persistent, efficient connection management is a critical thing on the server side.

## High-level design

You can ascertain, at least now, that WebSocket was considered as the main communication protocol between the client and the server because of its bidirectional communication approach. It is still equally necessary to tell that it is not only WebSocket that can be used. More often than not, most chat features (such as login, sign up, user profile, logout etc) can be handled with the normal request/response method over the most used HTTP. Let us try to go a notch higher and examine the high-level design of a chat system.

For convenience, the chat system can actually be broken down into three (3) main categories; Stateless services, third-party integration and Stateful services.

## Stateless Services

Stateless services are typical services that are people oriented and handle the request/response part. It is used to manage signup, login, user profile etc. You will agree that the signup, login and user profile are part of the most common features on many websites and apps.

The Stateless service is deeply rooted behind a load balancer whose main job is to route any request to the correct services using the request paths. The Stateless services can be monolithic (where the user interface and data access codes are combined into one program from a single platform) or individual microservices (where each service has its own database unlike monolithic). You, as a system designer, do not need to build much of these Stateless services by yourself, as there are many services in the market that can be integrated into your choosing. However, one thing that is worth talking about is the Service discovery. The main job of the service discovery is to assign a list of DNS host names of chat servers for the client.

## Stateful Service

The only stateful service is the chat service. It is called Stateful service because each of the clients is always able to maintain a secured and persistent network connection to a chat server. In a Stateful service, a client needs not switch to another chat server as long as the current server is still available. Server overloading is avoided since the service discovery can coordinate closely with the chat service. The deep dive step will discuss this in detail.

## Third-party integration

For a chat app, the push notification is one third-party integration you should consider. The push notification provides a means to tell app users that they have a new message inside the app even when the app is not active. Although, users that don't want the push notification can always disable the Push notification from Settings.

## Scalability

On a small scale, most or all of the services discussed above can actually fit in one server. Even at the chosen scale of design, it is always possible in theory to assign all apps users in a single cloud server. In your own case, at 5M concurrent users, assuming each user connection requires 10K of memory on the server, it only needs about 50GB of memory to accommodate all the connections in one box.

If you make a design where everything is accommodated in one server, this may pose a big red flag in the mind of your interviewer. No engineer would design such a scale with a single server.

However, it is okay to start with a single server design. Just ensure your interviewer knows this is a starting point. The various form of servers you can relate with in a chat systems are;

- Chat servers are for sending/receiving messages.
- Presence servers are for managing online/offline status.
- The API servers are the one that handle how users change profile, user login, sign up etc.
- Notification servers are used for sending push notifications.
- Finally, the chat history is stored by the key-value. Usually, when a user that has been offline before comes online, he/she will still be able to access all the previous chat history.

## Storage

Now that all servers are ready, services are running and third party integration (push notifications) has been put in place. The remaining technical stack is the data layer. It is important that you understand how to get the data layer correctly. Deciding on the right type of database to be used is an important requirement to figure out things easily. Let us clarify the data types and read/write patterns.

In a typical chat system, two types of data are common. You can have the **generic data** like the settings, user friend list, user profile etc. These data are always stored in relational databases. The second database is actually unique to chat systems: chat history data. It is expedient that you understand the read/write pattern.

- The amount of data consumed by chat systems is enormous. If you happen to see the amount of data WhatsApp processes per day, you will marvel.
- Users' psychology must be taken into cognizance as you will agree most users only access their recent chats. Old chats are barely accessed by users.
- Although, users are not likely to scroll and see old chats, but still, the data access layer must support features such as **jump to specific message, search, view your comments** and a lot of other features that can make chatting a convenient task for users.

Choosing the actual storage system that will support all of the use cases is pertinent. The key-value store is perfect because of the following reasons;

- Key-value stores enable easy horizontal scaling.
- Key-value stores give very low latency to access chat data. You can access as much data as possible within a few seconds.
- Key-value stores have been adopted by most of the earliest and prominent chat apps like Facebook messenger and Discord.

## Data models

You can take a good look at the one important data, which is the **message data;**

## Message table for 1 on 1 chat

The screenshot below shows the message table for a one-on-one chat. The **message_id** is the primary key which decides message sequence. The **created_id** cannot be relied upon while deciding the message sequence because you don't want to create two messages at the same time.

| message | |
| --- | --- |
| **message_id** | bigint |
| message_from | bigint |
| message_to | bitint |
| content | text |
| created_at | timestamp |

## Message table for a group chat

The image below depicts a message table for a group chat. The primary key here is (channel_id, message_id). Channel and group mean the same thing in this case. The channel_id is the partition key since all queries in a group chat work in a channel.

| group_message | |
| --- | --- |
| **channel_id** | bigint |
| **message_id** | bigint |
| user_id | bigint |
| content | text |
| created_at | timestamp |

# Message ID

The message _id is one very important topic you don't want to miss out. The message_id is the one that is responsible for the order of the messages. To ensure proper order of messages, the message_id must comply with the two requirements below;

- The message IDs must be totally unique.
- IDs should be such that new rows should have higher IDs than new rows. This means that you should be able to sort IDs by time.

These two requirements can be met by using a number of approaches; "auto_increment" keyword in MySql. But NoSQL databases do not give such a feature. Moreover, the second approach is to deploy a global 64-bit sequence number generator such as Snowflake. The final approach is to deploy a local sequence number generator. Local here means that IDs are only unique within a group.

## Step 3 - Design deep dive

During your interview, another important stage is where you dive deep into some components in the high-level design. Here, you can discuss service discovery, message inflow and online/offline presence indicators.

# Service discovery

It is true that geographical location and server stre-ngth actually determine the best chat server for users using chat apps. The main function of the service discovery is to recommend a better chat server for users. The Apache Zookeeper is a renowned open-source solution for service discovery. It helps register all the available chat servers and chooses the best chat server for a user based on predefined criteria.

# Message flows

It is exhilarating to understand the end-to-end flow of a chat system. Here, you will explore one-on-one chat flow, group chat flow and the message synchro-nization across multiple devices.

### 1 on 1 chat flow

*Let us check a chat system between two users (A and B) on two server mode; server 1 and server 2. What really happens can be summarized below;*

The figure explains what happens when User A sends a message to User B.

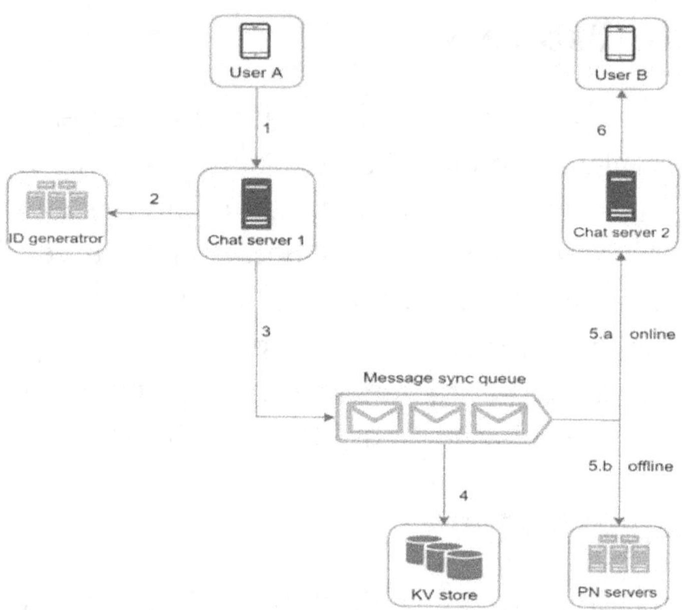


1. User A initiates a chat message to the Chat server 1.

2. Chat server 1 gets a message ID from the ID generator.

3. Chat server 1 forwards the message to the message sync queue.

4. The message is stored in a key-value store.

5a. If the User B is online, the message is automatically forwarded to Chat server 2 where the User B is connected.

5b. If the User B is not online, a push notification will be sent from push notification (PN) servers.

6. Chat server 2 sends the message to User B. A persistent WebSocket connection is established between User B and Chat server 2.

# Message synchronization across multiple devices

You cannot disregard the fact that some users have more than one device, ranging from Android phones, iPhones, PCs or tablets. There should be a way that they can use to sync messages across their various gadgets. Many users have multiple devices. We will explain how to sync messages across multiple devices. The figure shows an example of message synchronization.

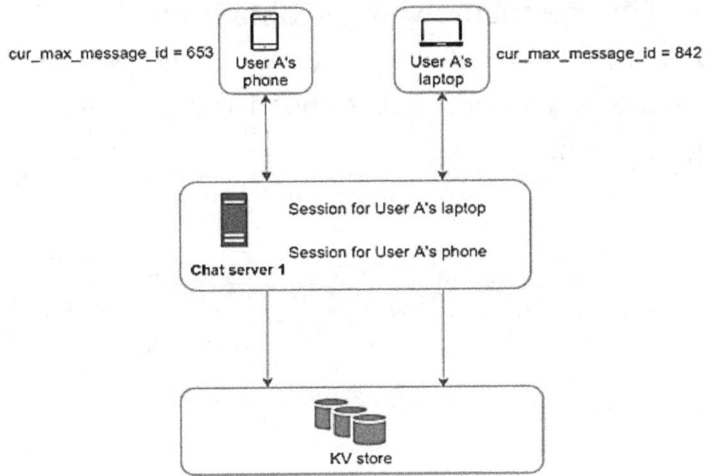


Let us say a particular user X has two devices: a PC and a phone. When User X logs in to the chat app with his phone, a WebSocket connection is established with chat server 1. Likewise, a connection is established between the PC and Chat server 1.

Each device (phone and PC) maintains a variable called cur_max_message_id, which helps to keep track of the latest message ID on the device. Messages that meet these two conditions will be categorized as new messages;

- The recipient ID is the same as the user ID that is currently logged in.
- The Message ID in the key-value store is greater than cur_max_message_id.

## Small group chat flow

When you compare what is obtainable in a Small group chat flow with what you have in the one-on-one chat system, you will see a much more complicated design system.

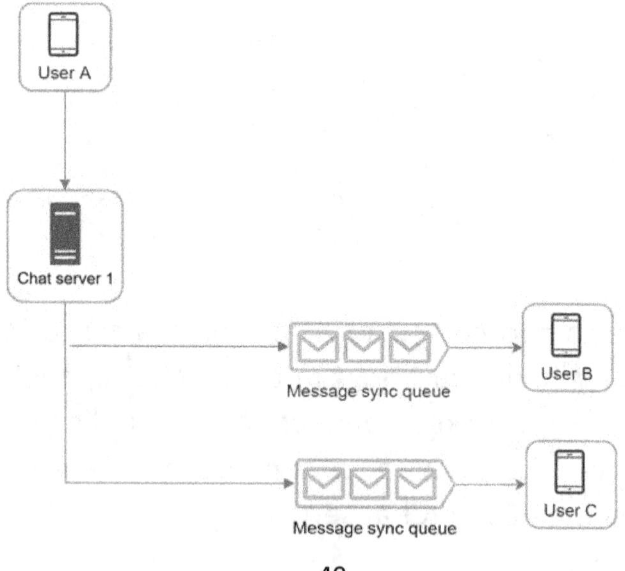

This is what happens when there are three members (A, B and C) in a group chat and one of them – say user A – send a message to the group;

- The message from user A is copied first to each of the group member's message sync queue; one will go to user B and the other will go to user B. Think of this message sync queue as an inbox for a recipient. This particular design choice is okay for small group chat (say between 5 to 10 members) because;
    - Message synchronization is easy, as each client involved only has to check its own message box to get the new message.
    - With a small group member, it becomes inexpensive to store a copy of a message in each of the recipient's inbox.

This type of system is used in WhatsApp where the admin cannot add more than 256 members. However, for a group chat with many users, it is not acceptable to store a message copy for each user.

If you observe things from the side of the recipient, you will notice that one recipient is able to receive messages from multiple users. Each recipient will have an inbox (message sync queue) which has messages from different senders.

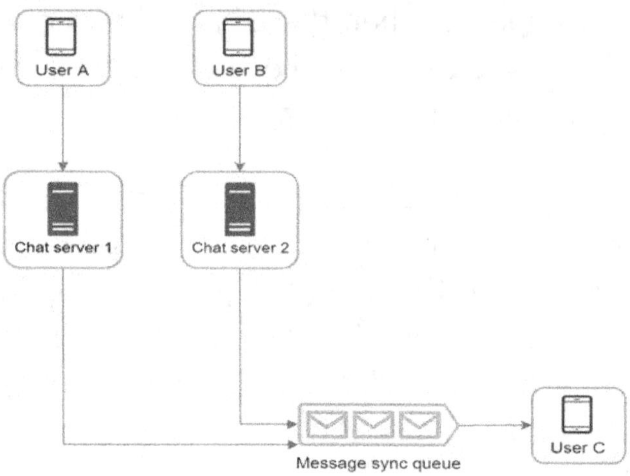



# Online presence

An online presence indicator is one important feature of a chat app, but that doesn't mean that a chat app that doesn't incorporate the online feature cannot be regarded as a chat app.  While using a chat app like WhatsApp, you will often see a green dot next to the username of a user or next to a user's profile picture which shows that the user is currently online. This part will talk about what happens in the background.

In the high-level design, presence servers are the ones responsible for managing online status and communication with clients through WebSocket. There are some flows that will ordinarily trigger online status change. You can take a look at each of them below;

# User login

The user login flow has been explained in the "Service Discovery" section. After a secured WebSocket connection has been established between the client and the real-time service, the user A's online status and last_active_at timestamp are automatically saved in the KV store. Presence indicator shows the user is online after she logs in.

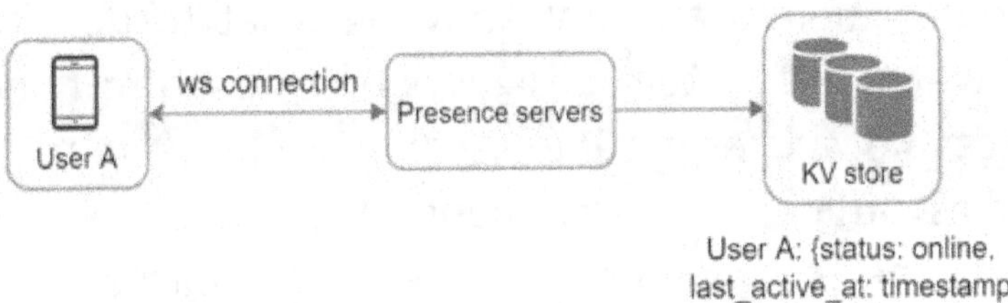


# User logout

When a user logs out of his/her chat app, it goes straight through the user logout flow as shown below. You can see as the online status has been changed to offline in the KV store and the presence indicator displays that the user is offline.

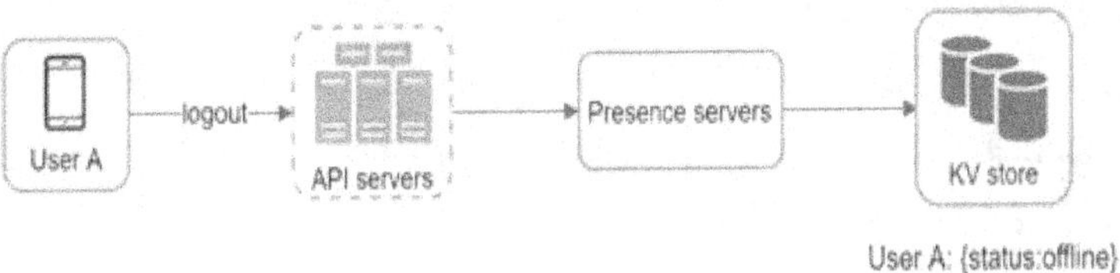

# User disconnection

While we can all wish that the internet connection is always consistent and stable. This, however, will not always be the case; hence, you need to address the issue of users getting disconnected either through bad service or other technical issues. When a particular user gets disconnected from the internet, the reliable connection between the server and the client that was previously enjoyed will be lost. This can make the user become clueless and not knowing what to do.  One bad way most system designers often used to handle the case of a user getting disconnected is to mark the user as offline and then change the status to online when the connection has been established. This approach has a major flaw. While it is not uncommon for users to disconnect and reconnect to the internet frequently in a short time, updating users' online status on each disconnect/reconnect will make the users' presence indicator changes quite often and this will result in a poor user experience.

We introduce a heartbeat mechanism to solve this problem. Periodically, an online client sends a heartbeat event to presence servers. If presence servers receive a heartbeat event within a certain time, say x seconds from the client, a user is considered as online. Otherwise, it is offline.

# Online Status fanout

When the online status of a user, say user A, changes, how do user A's friends know about this status change? The figure below explains how this will work. Presence servers deploy a publish-subscribe model, in which each friend pair maintains a channel. When the online status of user A changes, the presence server will publish this event to three channels; A-B, A-C and A-D. These three channels are subscribed by user B, C and D respectively. This makes it especially very easy for user A friends to get quick updates about user A online status update. The communication between clients and servers is through real-time WebSocket.

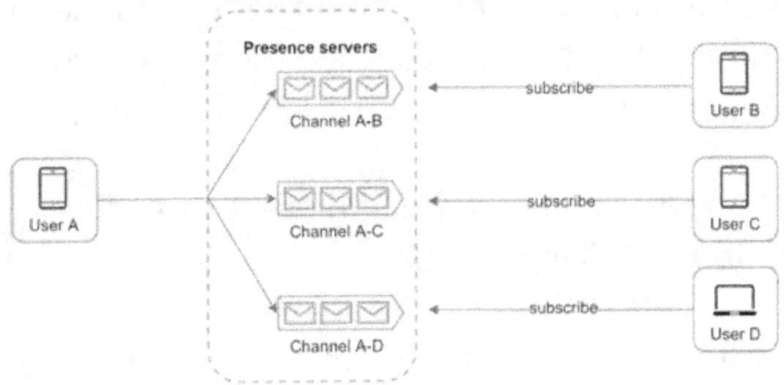


The above design is realizable if you are working with a small user group. For example, WeChat deploys a similar method because it doesn't really have a large user group (only 500 maximum). If you are working with a large group, it is actually very expensive and tedious to create a system that can inform all members about online status (presence). If a group has around 50,000 active members, each online status will produce 50,000 events. To mitigate this performance bottleneck, a possible solution is to fetch online status only when a user enters a group or manually refreshes the friend list.

## Step 4 - Wrap up

In this chapter, we presented a chat system architecture that supports both 1-to-1 chat and small group chat. WebSocket is used for real-time communication between the client and server. The chat system contains the following components: chat servers for real-time messaging, presence servers for managing online presence, push notification servers for sending push notifications, key-value stores for chat history persistence and API servers for other functionalities.

If you have extra time at the end of the interview, here are additional talking points:

- Extend the chat app to support media files such as photos and videos. Media files are significantly larger than text in size. Compression, cloud storage, and thumbnails are interesting topics to talk about.
- End-to-end encryption. Whatsapp supports end-to-end encryption for messages. Only the sender and the recipient can read messages.

- Caching messages on the client-side is effective to reduce the data transfer between the client and server.
- Improve load time. Slack built a geographically distributed network to cache users' data, channels, etc. for better load time.
- Error handling.
  - The chat server error. There might be hundreds of thousands, or even more persistent connections to a chat server. If a chat server goes offline, service discovery (Zookeeper) will provide a new chat server for clients to establish new connections with.
  - Message resent mechanism. Retry and queuing are common techniques for resending messages.

# CHAPTER THREE

## DESIGNING A URL SHORTENING SERVICE

There are many URL shortening services like TinyURL, bit.ly, goo.gl, qlink.me etc. But in this guide, you are going to be using the TinyURL shortening service.

## Why URL shortening service

You would agree that some website links are too long and complicated for ordinary users to relate with, and this will most times bore the user and might even discourage them from visiting that website. A supposedly longer website link can be shortened into a few words link that will take users directly to the same website as the longer version. So why having it longer when we can have it shorter and still serving the same purpose?

Essentially, you can use a URL shortening service to provide a short name alternative to a longer URL. These shortened aliases are called **short links.** Short links save users a lot of headache and spaces when typed, printed, tweeted or displayed. In order words, it is less likely for users to mistype a short URL.

For instance, if we shortened the link https://www.insightprovider/collection/page/4859890484764e89463w0746784/7346784947343/, you can get something like https://tinyurl.com/uy74pir which is a short alias for the longer web link above. Note that the web link inserted above is not a real web address as it is only used to show examples. TinyURL has a website https://tinyurl.com/ where you can use their service. All that you need to do is to copy your longer website link and then paste it inside the box shown below to shorten it.

**Welcome to TinyURL!™**

Are you sick of posting URLs in emails only to have it break when sent causing the recipient to have to cut and paste it back together? Then you've come to the right place. By entering in a URL in the text field below, we will create a tiny URL that *will not break in email postings* and *never expires*.

**Enter a long URL to make tiny:**

Make TinyURL!

Custom alias (optional):

https://tinyurl.com/

May contain letters, numbers, and dashes.

# System Functional Requirements

The URL shortening system should be one that meet the following requirements:

**Functional Requirements:**

1. The URL (which is the input) should be just a single original link and the system will provide a shortened version of the original link. The link will be short enough for users to be able to copy and paste easily into all of their applications.

2. When any user navigates the short link, the system will be able to direct them to the contents on the original link.

3. Users have liberty to choose and customize their short link without the system interfering in their choice.

4. The shortened link created will ordinarily expire after a set amount of time. Users should specify this time-frame.

**Non-Functional Requirements:**

1. The system should be stable and highly available. Why? Because if the system becomes interrupted, then all the shortened links created will die a natural death.

2. URL redirection (short link) should have short latency. This means that, with the short link, users should be able access the content on the large link within a short time. Much like saying the short link should be able to load fast even much better than the larger link from which it was created.

3. Shortened links should be one that cannot be guessed.

**Extended Requirements:**

1. Clicks Analytics; e.g., how many times a redirection occurred?
2. Provide a good API that is utilizable by third parties.

Capacity estimation

The system you are about to create will be read-heavy. You will have as many as possible redirection requests when compared to your new URL shortenings. Let us assume a 100:1 ratio between read and write.

**Traffic estimates:** Assuming, you plan to have 500M new URL shortenings per month, with 100:1 read/write ratio, you can be expecting 50B redirections during this same period:

100 * 500M => 50B

You can estimate the Queries Per Second (QPS) for the system, which is the New URLs shortenings per second:

500 million / (30 days * 24 hours * 3600 seconds) = ~200 URLs/s

On a 100:1 read/write ratio, the URLs redirections per second will be: 100 * 200 URLs/s = 20K/s

**Storage estimates:** Let us assume that you store every URL shortening request (and associated shortened link) for a period of 5 years, and you are expecting to have 500M new URLs every month, the total number of items you can be planning to store will be;

500 million * 5 years * 12 months = 30 billion

On an assumption that each of the item stored will be 500 bytes approximately, you will need 15TB of total storage space;

30 billion * 500 bytes = 15 TB

**Bandwidth estimates:** For the write requests, since you are planning 200 new URLs every second, the total incoming data for your service will be 100KB per second:

200 * 500 bytes = 100 KB/s

For the read requests, since you are expecting, on the average, ~20K URLs redirects every second, the total outgoing data for your service would be 10MB per second:

20K * 500 bytes = ~10 MB/s

**Memory estimates:** If you plan to cache some of the hot URLs that are frequently accessed, how much memory will you need to store them? If you follow the 80-20 rule, meaning 20% of URLs bring 80% of traffic, you would like to cache these 20% hot URLs.

Since you have 20K requests per second, you are planning to be having 1.7 billion requests per day:

20K * 3600 seconds * 24 hours = ~1.7 billion

To cache 20% of these requests, you will require 170GB of memory.

0.2 * 1.7 billion * 500 bytes = ~170GB

One thing you need to understand here is that since there will be as many as possible duplicate requests (of the same URL), your actual memory usage will be less than 170GB.

## API design

The System's API can be defined by using the SOAP or REST API. Two types of APIs can be designed here; create URL API and the delete URL API.

### createURL

The API below can be used to create a shortened link;

```
createURL(api_dev_key,
          original_url,
          custom_alias=None,
          expire_date=None)
```

Let us define each of the parameter in the API;

**Parameters:**

- **api_dev_key (string):** This represents the API developer key of a registered   account. This key will be used to limit the number of user requests and also identify the users based on their allocated quota.
- **original_url (string):** This represents the original URL that a user wants to     shorten.
- **custom_alias (string):** This represents the optional custom key for the URL.
- **user_name (string):** Optional username that will be used in the encoding.
- **expire_date (string):** This stands for the optional expiration date for the shortened URL.

**Return value:** (string)

A successful insertion will return the shortened URL; if not, it brings an error code.

**deleteURL**

The API is as well necessary to delete the shortened link registered.

```
deleteURL(api_dev_key, url_key)
```

- **api_dev_key (string):** This is the API developer key of the registered user account.
- **url_key (string):** Represents the shortened link.

**Return value (string):**
- The shortened link will be deleted if successful. A successful deletion will bring "URL removed."

- An error code is displayed if it fails.

**How do we detect and prevent abuse?** A hacker posing as a user can jeopardize your URL shortening website by using up all the URL keys in your current design. Our concern is not even how this is possible but how to prevent unwarranted attacks like this. To totally eliminate abuse, you can limit users through their api_dev_key. Each api_dev_key can actually be limited to a specific number of URL creations and redirections per some time period (which may be set to a different duration per developer key).

# Database design

The following are the things you must understand about the data that needs to be stored;

- System should be one that can store billions of records.

- Each of the stored objects is small (less than 1K).

- No relationship whatsoever between each saved record. The only thing the system should do is to store which user created a URL.

- The system should be heavily read.

**Database schema:**

We will need 2 main tables: one table will store the URL information and the second table will store the data of the user who requests a short link.

| URL | |
|---|---|
| PK | **Hash: varchar(16)** |
| | OriginalURL: varchar(512) |
| | CreationDate: datetime |
| | ExpirationDate: datatime |
| | UserID: int |

| User | |
|---|---|
| PK | **UserID: int** |
| | Name: varchar(20) |
| | Email: varchar(32) |
| | CreationDate: datetime |
| | LastLogin: datatime |

# What kind of database should we use?

Since there is no correlation between users stored in the database, and also billions of users have to be saved, you can use a NoSQL  key-value like Cassandra and DynamoDB. It is always easier to scale a NoSQL key-value.

**Basic System Design and Algorithm#**

The basic essence of a system design like the one you are doing is to create a short and unique link from a long original URL.

If, for instance, you obtained a short link "[http://tinyurl.com/jlg8zpc](http://tinyurl.com/jlg8zpc)" from a very long URL when you used the TinyURL platform, the last seven (7) characters of the shirt link above is what you are about to generate. There are two likely ways of solving this;

**a. Encoding actual URL #**

You can create some hash functions (e.g. MD5 or SHA256, etc.) that can be used to hash the given URL. Then hash can then be encoded for displaying. This encoding could be base 36 (a-z ,0-9) or base 62 (A-Z, a-z, 0-9) a base 64 encoding can also be used if you managed to add '+' and '/.'

One reasonable question that should be coming to your mind right now is the length of the short keys to be used. Should it be 6 characters long, 8 characters or even 10 characters?

If you are working with a base64 encoding, using a 6 letters long key would result in 64^6 = ~68.7 billion possible strings, and an 8 letters long key would result in 64^8 = ~281 trillion possible strings

With the 68.7B unique strings, you can assume that six letter keys would be enough for the system.

If you are using the MD5 algorithm as your hash function, you will have a 128-bit hash value. After base64 encoding, you will have a string having more than 21 characters (since each base64 character encodes 6 bits of the hash value). This will result in eight (8) characters per short key. How then can you choose your short keys? You can actually use the first 6 or 8 characters for your key. Although, this might lead to key duplication but you can resolve this by selecting some other characters out of the strings or swapping some characters with another.

# Analyzing some issues with your design

The following couple of issues can be identified with the encoding scheme you used above;

1. In a case that multiple users enter the same URL, the same short link might be assigned to them which is not okay.
2. What if some parts of the URL are URL-encoded? Forinstance, http://www. userdeisgn.pr/distributed .php?id=design,and http://www.userdesign.pr/dist ributed.php%3Fid%3Ddesign look alike but the only difference is the URL encoding.

**You can solve these issues:** You can dedicate an increasing sequence number to each input URL to create uniqueness, and then make a hash of it. You don't necessarily need to save this sequence in the database. One possible problem with an approach like this could be an ever-increasing number of numbers. The service performance is also affected when you assign an increasing number of sequences.

Another solution could be to assign user id (which should, of course, be unique) to the input URL. However, if this user has not signed in, you will need to request the user to select a uniqueness key. Even when this has been done, there is no guarantee that conflict will not result anytime, but if it does, you would need to keep creating a key until you get a unique key.

## b. Generating keys offline

It is easier to use a standalone **Key Generation Service (KGS)** capable of  generating unique random six-letter strings at any time and saves them in a database (you can call this database key-DB). This means that anytime you want to shorten a particular link, you only have to pick from one of the keys you have generated with a Key Generation Service and deploy it. This method will not only make your work fast but also very simple and easy. Furthermore, this method is devoid of key duplication nor URL encoding. The Key Generation Service will always ensure that the keys you used inside the key-DB are all unique.

**Key concurrency can occur and you must avoid it:** Once you have successfully used a key, you will need to mark it in the database to make sure that the key doesn't get reused. If multiple servers are reading your keys concurrently, you can have a case where two or more servers will be trying to read the same key from the database.  If the concurrency problem occurs in the design, how best can you solve it?

Servers can deploy the Key Generation Service to mark/read keys in the database.  The KGS can have two tables that can be used to store keys: one table for keys that have not been used yet, and another table for all the keys that you have used. Once the KGS assigns a particular key, it will move the assigned key to the table (the one you created for used keys). The Key Generation Service (KGS) can as well save some keys in its memory and these keys will be provided anytime a server needs them.

For the purpose of simplicity, once KGS loads some keys in memory, it can take them to the used keys table. This ensures that each server gets unique keys. If KGS could not complete the process of loading keys to some servers due to one reason or another, the remaining keys will go to waste – which is not bad yet considering the multitude of keys that can be regenerated from the KGS once it is back on track.

KGS also needs to ensure that it does not assign the same key to multiple servers. For this, it must be able to synchronize (or get a lock on) the data structure holding the keys before removing keys from it and assigning them to a server.

**What would be the key-DB size?** If you are using the base64 encoding, you can make 68.7B unique six letters keys. If we only need one byte to save one alphanumeric character, you will be able to store all these keys in:

6 (characters per key) * 68.7B (unique keys) = 412 GB.

**Is KGS not a single point of failure?** Yes, it is. You can solve this problem by having a standby replica of Key Generation Service. This means that whenever the primary server is stopped (for one reason or another), the standby server will mount position and start the process of generating and providing keys.

**Can each app server cache some keys from key-DB?** Of course, this will most times, even, speed up things. Although, if the application server gets disconnected before it uses up all the keys, you will lose all the keys. This is not too bad since you can have about 68 billion unique 6 letter keys.

**How would we perform a key lookup?** You will be able to look up the keys in your database to access the complete URL. If it is available in the database DB, prompt an "HTTP 302 Redirect" status back to the browser, passing the saved URL in the "Location" field of the request. If the key is not available in the system, prompt an "HTTP 404 Not Found" status or take the user back to the homepage.

**Should a size limit be imposed on custom aliases?** The service you created supports custom aliases. Users can select any 'key' they want, but it is not mandatory for them to provide a custom alias. But if you want to have a consistent URL database, it is only proper to impose a size limit on a custom alias.

## Data Partitioning and Replication

You will be required to partition your database to scale out your DB. This is so that the DB can store information for billions of web links. The partitioning scheme that will be appropriate here is the one that can divide and store data into different DB servers.

1. **Range Based Partitioning:** The first letter of the hash key can be a clue to store URLs in separate partitions. You can store all URLs that begin with letter "B" (and "b") in one partition, and then save

those that begin with letter "J" in another partition and then go on like this. This method is referred to as **Range Based Partitioning.** You can even mix some specific letters that usually occur less frequently into one database partition. You can even come up with a static partitioning method so URLs can be stored or searched in a predictable way. One main flaw of this system is that unbalanced DB servers can result.

2. **Hash-Based Partitioning:** In this method, you take a hash of the object you are storing. You can then go ahead to calculate which partition to use based on the hash. In your case, you can take the hash of the 'key' or the short link to know the partition in which you can store the data object. The hashing function will randomly share URLs into different partitions (e.g., your hashing function can usually map any 'key' to a number between [1...256]), and this number will stand for the partition in which you store your object. This method can still cause overloaded partitions, which you can solve by using Consistent Hashing.

# Cache

URLs that are accessed frequently can be cached. Some off-the-shelf solutions, like **Memcached,** can be adapted to store complete URLs with their various hashes. The application servers can check if the cache contains the desired URL before the application spirals into backend storage.

**How much cache memory is advisable to have?** You can begin with 20% of daily traffic and then adjust later based on clients' usage pattern. As previously estimated, about 170GB memory is needed to cache 20% of daily traffic. Nowadays, there are servers that can have 256GB memory and all the cache can easily be assembled into one machine.

**Which cache eviction policy would fit your needs better?** When the cache has been fully occupied, and you want to replace a link with a newer URL, how then would you choose? You can consider using Least Recently Used (LRU) as a standard policy for your system. This policy involves discarding, first, the least recently used URL. You can use a Linked Hash Map or a similar data structure to store your URLs and Hashes, which can help keep track of the URLs that have been recently accessed. If you want to further increase the efficiency, you can replicate the caching servers to distribute the load between them.

**How can each cache replica be updated?** Whenever a server is missed, the server will automatically hit a backend database. Once this occurs, the cache can be updated and the new entry will be passed to all the cache replicas. Each replica will be able to update its cache by inserting the new entry. If a replica has that entry already, it can simply ignore it.

## Load Balancer (LB)

A load-balancing layer can be added at three different places in the system;

1. Between Application servers and Clients.
2. Between database servers and Application Servers.
3. Between Application Servers and Cache servers

Initially, a simple Round Robin approach that distributes incoming requests equally among backend servers can be used. This Load Balancer is very easy to implement and will not introduce any overhead. Another importance of this approach is that if a server is not active, the Load Balancer will bring it out of the rotation and will cease to send any traffic to it.

One problem with Round Robin Load Balancer is that the server load is not taken into consideration. If a server is slow or has been overloaded, the Load Balancer will not desist from sending new requests to the server. To work around this, a more robust LB solution can be put in place that will query the backend server periodically about its load and then adjusts traffic based on that.

## Purging or DB cleanup

Making a decision in your design about whether all users' entries should be saved forever or deleted after some time is also important. If a particular user specified expiration time has been exceeded, what should happen to the user's link?

If you plan to only remove expired links by searching for them, the database will not have rest. Instead, you can remove an expired link slowly and carry out a lazy cleanup. The service is to ensure that only links that are expired will be deleted, even though some expired links can still be active but will never be made available to the user again.

- Anytime a particular user tries to use an expired link, the link can be deleted and the user will be prompted with an error.

- You can have a separate Cleanup service in place that can be running periodically to delete expired links from the storage and cache. This service is not really a heavy one and should only be run when the user traffic is low or expected to be low.

- You can set a default time for each created link to expire (2 or 3 years).

- Once an expired link has been removed, the key can be inserted back in the key-DB to be reused.

- Should links that have not been opened within some period of time (say 6 months) be deleted? Well, there are many storage capacities to go around, you can choose to leave those links alone.

# Telemetry

How many times a particular short URL has been used, what were the locations of each user? How should this information be stored?

You can actually agree that there are some statistics that are worth tracking: country of the user, date and time the user uses the link, the actual web page that refers the click, and the browser, or platform from which the user was able to access the page.

# Security and Permission

Can users create some private URLs or enable some particular set of users to access a URL?

The information level (be private or public) can be stored with each URL in the database. A separate table can equally be created that can store Users' IDs that have access to view a specific URL. If a particular user does not have permission and tries to access a specific URL, the system can send an error (HTTP 401) back. Given that the data are being stored in a NoSQL wide-column database, like Cassandra, the key for the table scoring permission will be the 'Hash' or the key that was generated by the KGS. The columns will save the ID of the users (for only those users that have permission to view the URL).

# CHAPTER FOUR

## DESIGNING A VIDEO STREAMING PLATFORM LIKE YOUTUBE

As part of your System Design Interview, you can be requested to design YouTube. The same way you design YouTube is the same way you will design other popular video streaming platforms like Netflix and Hulu.

YouTube, in recent time, has become the largest video streaming platform allowing content creators of all kinds to upload their videos for viewers' consumption. Although, to viewers, the outlook and the appearance of YouTube might look simple; to them it is just another video streaming where they can get to watch their favorite YouTuber and learn. But you should of course understand more than this because there are myriads of complex technologies embedded in the design of YouTube and that is what we are going to be taking a look at in this section.

## Getting to understand the problem and establish your design scope

YouTube is not solely for watching video, there are lots more you can do on the popular video streaming platform. For instance, you can; share a video, subscribe to premium, save a video to your playlist, comment on a video, like a video, down-vote a video and other things. Although it is not possible to design and talk about everything during your 45 minutes SDI, this is why it is pertinent that you enquire what the interviewer wants from you so that you will be able to narrow it down. In this stage, the following conversation can ensue between you and your interviewer;

**You:** What features in the design are important?
**Interviewer:** Users should be able to watch and upload video.

**You:** Is it YouTube for mobile only, web only or both?

**Interviewer:** YouTube must be able to run on mobile apps, smart TV and web browsers.

**You:** What is the minimum Daily active user?
**Interviewer:** 5 million

**You:** What is the average daily time spent on the product?

**Interviewer:** 30 minutes.

**You:** Will the product support international users?

**Interviewer:** Yes, it must cover a larger percentage of international users.

**You:** Can you tell me about the video resolution that can be supported on the product?

**Interviewer:** The system should be one that accepts most of the video formats and resolutions.

**You:** Is there any encryption?

**Interviewer:** Yes

**You:** Will the video have specific file size requirements?

**Interviewer:** Small and medium size video should be the point of focus. The maximum video size allowed is 1GB.

**You:** Can any of the existing cloud infrastructure provided by Google, Microsoft or Amazon be leveraged in this product?

**Interviewer:** Yes, you can leverage on some of the existing infrastructure provided by those websites.

In the section, your focus is on designing a video streaming service that has the following features;

- Unhindered ability to upload videos fast.
- Users should be able to stream video easily without any hindrance.
- Users must be able to change video quality.
- The cost of infrastructure must not be too expensive.
- High scalability, availability, and reliability requirements
- It must support users on; mobile apps, smart TV and web browsers.

## Estimation

The following product estimations are just for the purpose of this guide. In a real life interview, it is important you communicate with your interviewers to be on the same page about how the product's estimation is expected to be done.

- Assume this particular video streaming platform will have 5 million daily active users (DAU).
- Each user watches 5 videos per day.
- 10% of users post 1 video per day.
- The average size of each video is 300 MB.
- Total storage space needed daily: 5 million * 10% * 300 MB = 150TB
- CDN cost.

- When cloud CDN serves a video, you will be charged for data transferred out of the CDN.
  - You can use Amazon's CDN CloudFront for cost estimation.  Assume that 100% of the traffic is served from the United States. The average cost per GB is $0.02. For simplicity, you can only estimate the cost of video streaming.
  - 5 million * 5 videos * 0.3GB * $0.02 = $150,000 per day.

From this small calculation, it is visible that serving videos from the CDN actually costs more. Even though the cloud providers might offer a lower CDN cost for big customers, this is still a huge cost to bear. In the deep dive section, the various ways of reducing CDN cost will be discussed.

## Propose high-level design and get buy-in

As observed previously, the interviewer recommended using existing cloud services from Amazon instead of building the whole product from scratch. The CDN and blob storage are the cloud services that will be leveraged here. The reasons you are not likely to build the whole product from the scratch are;

- System design interviews are not exactly about building everything from scratch. Within the short time frame that you have, talking about the right technology to get the job done is actually more important and beneficial than explaining how the technology works in detail. For example, mentioning blob storage for storing source videos is enough for your interviewer. When you start talking about everything behind the CDN or blob storage might not be needed and can be regarded as an overkill.

- Building a scalable blob storage or CDN is very complex and costly. Even large companies like Netflix or Facebook do not build everything themselves. Netflix leverages Amazon's cloud services, and Facebook deploys Akamai's CDN.

At the high-level, the system comprises three components as shown below;

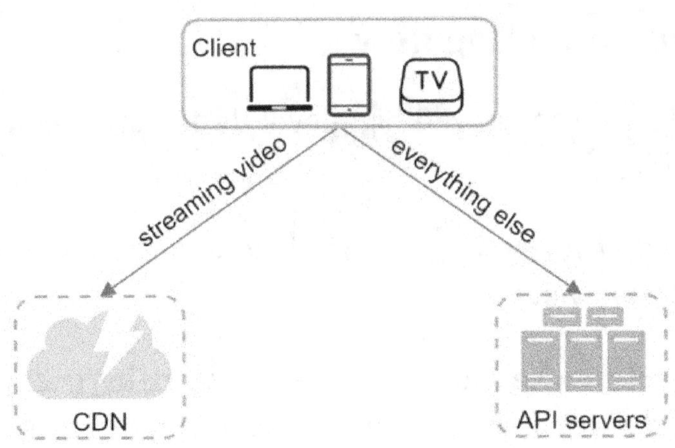


**Client**: YouTube videos can be watched on your computer, mobile devices and Smart televisions.

**CDN**: Videos are stored in CDN. When you click play in a video, the video will be streamed from the CDN.

**API servers**: The only thing that does not go through the API servers is the video streaming. This features generating video upload URL, user signup, updating cache and metabase data, feed recommendation etc.

During the question & answer part of the interview, you will notice that the interviewer showed interest in the two flows below;

- Video uploading flow
- Video streaming flow

We will examine the high-level design for each of them below;

## Video uploading flow

The figure displays the high-level design for the video uploading.

The high-level design for the video uploading consists of the following;

- **User:** The video can be watched by users on devices like computer, mobile phone, or smart TV.
- **Load balancer:** A load balancer will assist in distributing requests evenly among API servers.

- **API servers:** All of the user requests go straight through the API servers except video streaming.
- **Metadata DB:** Video metadata will be stored in Metadata DB. It is replicated to conform to performance and high availability requirements.
- **Metadata cache:** User objects and video metadata are cached for good performance.
- **Original storage:** A blob storage system can be used to store original videos.
- **Transcoding servers:** Video transcoding can also be called video encoding. It is the act of converting a video format to another video format (MPEG, HLS, etc), which give the best video streams possible for different devices and bandwidth capabilities.
- **Transcoded storage:** It is a blob storage that stores transcoded video files.
- **CDN:** Videos are cached in CDN. When you tap on the play button, the video will be streamed from the CDN.
- **Completion queue:** This is a message queue that saves information about video transcoding completion events.
- **Completion handler:** This consists of a list of workers that pull event data from the completion queue and update metadata cache and database.

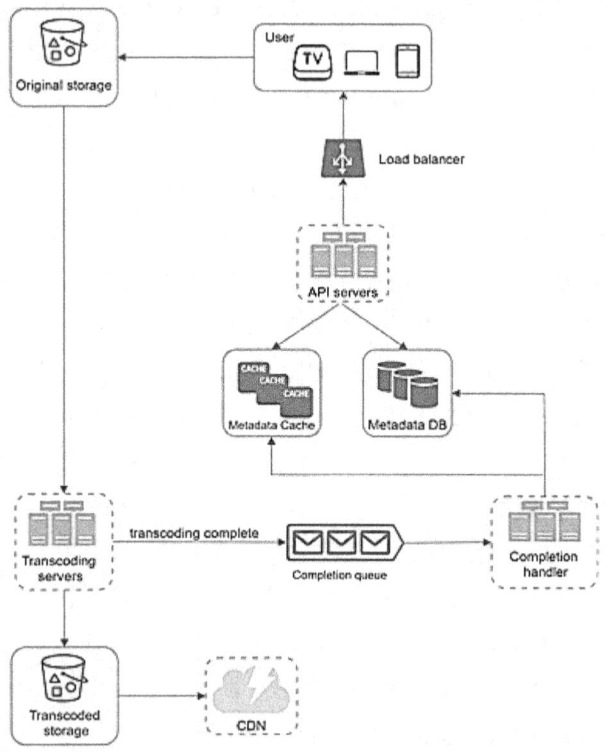


Now that you have understood each component individually, you can examine how the video uploading flow actually works. The flow can be broken down into two processes running in parallel.

- Upload the actual video.
- Update video metadata. Metadata features information about video size, URL, format, resolution, user info, etc.

***Flow a: upload the actual video***

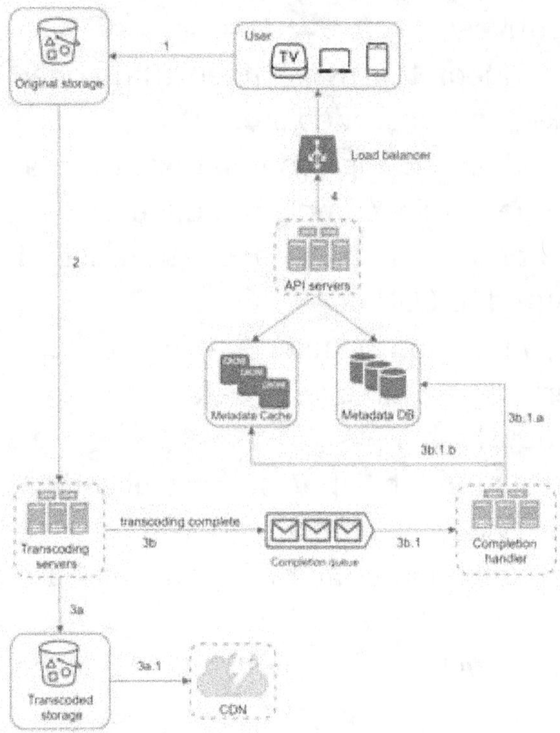

The above figure displays how you upload the actual video. The explanation of the flow chart is as shown below;

- 1. Videos are uploaded to the original storage.
- 2. The videos from the original storage are fetch from the transcoding servers and the transcoding process begins.

- 3. Once the transcoding process has been completed, the two processes below will be carried out consecutively;
    - ○ 3a. Videos that have been transcoded are taken to transcoded storage.
    - ○ 3b. Transcoding completion events are queued in the completion queue.
  - 3a.1. Videos that have been transcoded are distributed to CDN.
  - 3b.1. Completion handler features a bunch of workers that pull event data from the que continuously.
  - 3b.1.a. and 3b.1.b. Upon successful completion of the video transcoding, the completion handler will update the metadata database and cache.
- 4. API servers will tell the client that the video has been uploaded successfully and the video can now be streamed.

### *Flow b: update the metadata*

While a file is being uploaded to the original storage, the client will send a request in parallel to update the video metadata as displayed in the figure below. The request features video metadata, including the name of the file, size, format, etc. API servers update the metadata cache and database.

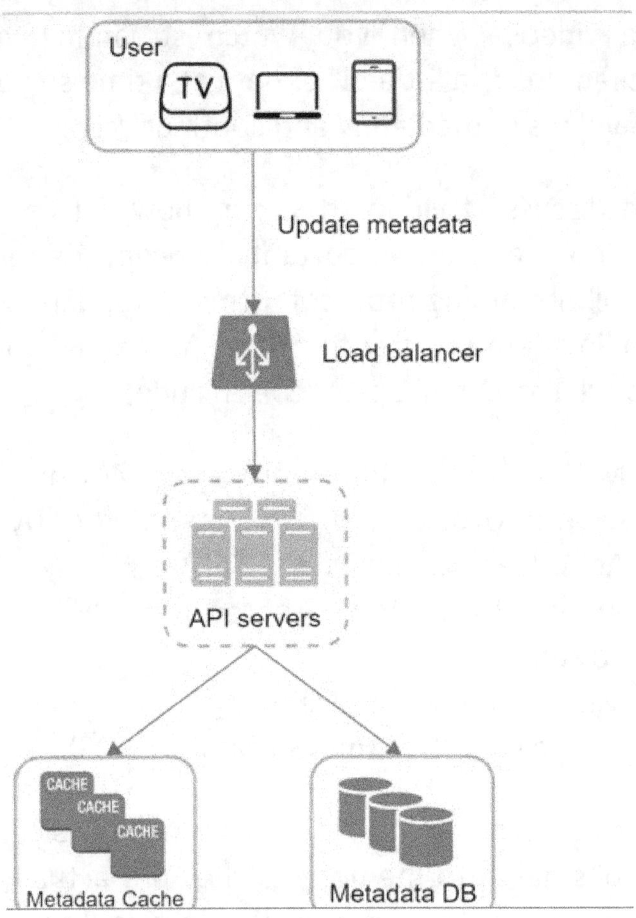



# Video streaming flow

Whenever you tap to play a video on YouTube, it will normally start streaming immediately and you never have to wait until the whole video has been downloaded. Downloading means, the whole video has been copied to your device, while streaming means that your device (Android, iPhone, tablet or PC) continuously receives video streams from remote source videos. When you watch streaming videos, your client loads a little bit of data at a time so you can watch videos immediately and continuously.

Before discussing video streaming flow, let us take a good look at an important concept: streaming protocol. Streaming protocol forms a standard way of controlling data transfer for video streaming. Some of the popular streaming protocols include;

- MPEG–DASH. MPEG represents "Moving Picture Experts Group" and DASH stands for "Dynamic Adaptive Streaming over HTTP".
- Apple HLS. HLS represents "HTTP Live Streaming".
- Microsoft Smooth Streaming.
- Adobe HTTP Dynamic Streaming (HDS).

You don't necessarily have to commit the streaming protocol's name to memory as they are actually low-level details that need specific domain knowledge. One very important thing is to know that different streaming protocols actually support different video encodings and playback players. Upon designing a video streaming service, you will need to choose the right streaming protocol that can support your use case.

Videos are normally streamed directly from CDN. The edge server that is very close to you at that moment will be the one to deliver the video. Hence, there is very little latency.

## Design deep dive

As you have seen in the high-level design, the whole system is broken down in two parts: video uploading flow and video streaming flow. In this section, both of the flows will be refined with necessary optimizations and error handling mechanisms will be introduced.

## Video transcoding

When you shoot a video, your device (usually a phone or camera) appends a video format for the video file. If you want your video to be able to play perfectly on other devices, you must encode the video into compatible bitrates and formats. Bitrate refers to the rate at which bits are processed over time. A higher bitrate literally means higher video quality. A video with high bitrate will need more processing power and fast internet speed.

The following are the importance of video transcoding;

- Raw video uses large amounts of storage space. A 1hr video shot at 60 fps can consume a few hundred GB of space.

- Many devices and browsers only play certain types of video formats. Hence, it is imperative you encode a video to different formats for compatibility reasons.
- Video encoding makes sure users are able to watch high-quality videos while still maintaining smooth playback. It will always be a good idea to bring higher resolution video to users who have high network bandwidth and lower resolution video to users with low bandwidth.
- Network conditions can change, especially on mobile devices. To ensure a video is played continuously, switching video quality automatically or manually based on network conditions is essential for smooth user experience.

More than one type of encoding formats are available; however, most of them contain two parts:

- **Container:** This is like a container that contains the video file, audio, and metadata. You can tell the container format by the file extension, such as .avi, .mov, or .mp4.
- **Codecs:** These are compression and decompression algorithms aim to lower the size of the video while still preserving the quality of the video. The video codecs that are mostly used include; H.264, VP9, and HEVC.

# Safety optimization: protect your videos

A lot of YouTube video creators are scared of sharing their videos online because of video theft. Imagine someone else taking credit for their sweat. The following options are safe if you are planning to protect your copyrighted video from theft;

- Digital rights management (DRM) systems: The three main DRM systems recognized are Apple FairPlay, Google Widevine, and Microsoft Play-Ready.
- AES encryption: For safety purposes, you can encrypt your video and then configure an authorization policy. The video you encrypted will only be decrypted upon playback. This will ensure that only authorized viewers can watch an encrypted video.
- Visual watermarking: A watermark is like an image overlay across the video identifying you as the sole owner of the video. The name can be the name of your business or logo of your company.

## Cost-saving optimization

CDN is an important part of the system. It makes fast video delivery possible on a global scale. However, having done some serious back of the envelope calculations, you have seen that CDN is actually expensive, especially when you are working with a large data size. How then can the cost be reduced?

Previous understanding proved that YouTube video streams follow long-tail distribution. What this means is that a few popular videos are accessed frequently while many others have little or no viewers at all. Based on this observation, few optimizations can be implemented to solve this;

1. Most popular videos should only be served from the CDN and other videos should be served from the high capacity storage server.

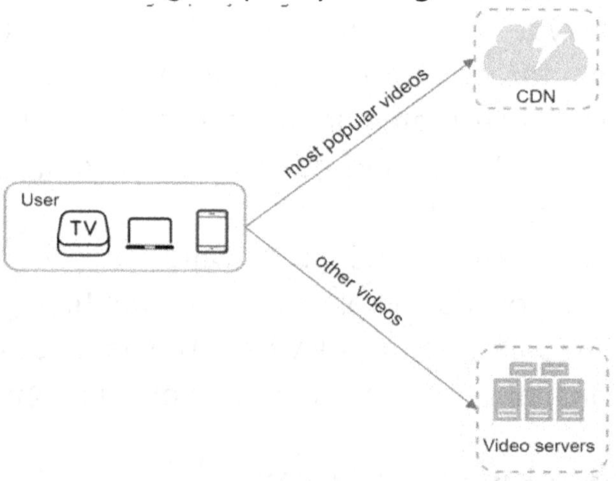


2. For contents that are considered less popular, there may not be any need to store many encoded video versions. Short videos can be encoded on demand.
3. Some videos are region specific, meaning that they are only popular in some regions. You don't need

to distribute these videos in regions where they are perceived not to be popular.

4. You can take the challenge of building your own CDN just like Netflix and then partner with Internet Service Providers (ISPs). Although, building your own CDN is demanding and a hard task to complete, however this can be perfect if your company is a large streaming company just like Netflix. By partnering with ISPs, you can improve viewing experience and also lower bandwidth charges.

All of these video optimizations are based on content popularity, video size, user access pattern etc. It is good to analyze historical viewing patterns before you implement any optimization.

**Error handling**

For a large-scale system, system errors cannot be avoided. If you are thinking of building a good system that is fault-tolerant, then you need to have a system in place that can handle errors, and can get the system back on track if an error does occur. Two types of errors can be recognized in this case;

- **Recoverable error:** Errors like video segment fails to transcode is a recoverable error. The troubleshooting idea is to try the operation more than once. If the task still continues to fail and the system cannot really recover the operation after many trials, then the system will bring a proper error code to the operator.

- **Non-recoverable error:** For errors that are considered non-recoverable such as malformed video format, the system will stop the running tasks associated with the video and then prompt a proper error code to the client.

Typical errors for each system component can be discussed;

- **Upload error:** Retry the operation a few times.
- **Transcoding error:** Retry a couple of times.
- **Preprocessor error:** Regenerate DAG diagram
- **DAG scheduler error:** Reschedule a task
- **Resource manager queue down:** Deploy a replica
- **Task worker down:** Retry the task on a new worker
- **API server down:** API servers are stateless so requests will be directed to a different API server.
- **Metadata cache server down:** Data is replicated multiple times. If one node goes down, you can still access other nodes to fetch data. We can bring up a new cache server to replace the dead one.

# Wrap up

In this chapter, you have seen the architecture design for a video streaming service like YouTube. If you still have extra time at the end of your interview, here are some extra ideas;

- Scale the API tier: Scaling API tier horizontally is easy since API servers are stateless.
- Scale the database: You can discuss some things about database replication and sharding.
- Live streaming: This entails how a video is recorded and broadcasted in real time. Although the system has not been designed specifically for live streaming, live streaming and non-live streaming have some similarities in that both actually require uploading, encoding, and streaming. The notable differences include:
  - Live streaming features a higher latency requirement, so it might require a different streaming protocol.
  - Live streaming has a lower requirement for parallelism since small amounts of data are already processed in real-time.
  - Live streaming requires different sets of error handling. Any error handling that takes too much time is not acceptable.
  - Video takedowns: Any video that violate some illegal acts, copyrights, or pornography will be

deleted. Some of these videos are often discovered during the process of uploading the video while a few others are always discovered through flagging by users.

# CHAPTER FIVE

## DESIGNING DROPBOX

Dropbox is a popular file hosting service where users get to upload their files for safe and easy download by other users. Now, as part of your preparation for your next System Design Interview, you are about to see the exclusive technology that runs beneath the working of the popular file hosting service called Dropbox. Another common example of a file hosting service is the Google Doc. In this chapter, you will dive into the design of a Dropbox or Google Drive.

Likewise, we are not designing our own cloud storage platform in this guide as it is not necessary and an SDI will not prompt you to design one. We will rather use the Amazon cloud storage service or any other cloud storage service.

## Discuss About the Core Features

One good trait you can inculcate at the interview is to ask questions. Enquire you're your interviewer what they are expecting from you and you should never assume anything unless you are asked to do so. By asking questions, you will be able to understand the scope of the system. This will go a long way to clear all doubts. Here, you should begin with the core features of the Dropbox or Google Drive you are asked to design; what are the features that are expected in the design, how many users on the average per day and a lot of other questions. In case the interviewer wants you to add more features, they will let you know later as the interview proceeds. The interviewer, after series of initial chats, let you understand the features to be expected in the product design should have the following menus;

- Users should be able to upload/download on the platform. Likewise, there should be a menu for updating and deleting of files.
- File versioning (History of updates)
- File and folder sync
- Traffic: - 12+ million active users. – should be able to cover 100 million requests per day with many reads and writes.

## Discuss the Problem Statement

Many people have the wrong believe about what goes beneath the Dropbox design. To them, Dropbox is all about using some cloud services to host the files, upload their documents on the platform, and then download the documents anytime they wish. Nevertheless, this is not the way these things actually work. The prevalent bone of contention is mostly about **where and how to save the files.** Let us assume that you plan to share a certain file with a known or unknown file size and you then proceed to upload your file into the cloud, of course it looks simple this way until you have to make an update to the file; as updating the file by editing the file and then upload it again is not exactly a good idea. The reason for this can be explained in terms of;

- **More bandwidth and cloud space utilization:** To provide a full account and history of the files you will need to save the multiple versions of the files. This needs more bandwidth and more file space in the cloud. Backing up and transferring the whole file like this needs more space which is not a good thing.

- **Latency or Concurrency Utilization:** Time optimization is also a hard thing to accomplish, as more time will be needed to upload one file as a whole. Likewise, uploading files concurrently using multiple threads or processes is not a welcome idea.

## Discuss the Solution (High-Level Solution)

To get rid of the issues discussed above, it is possible we break files into many chunks. There won't be any need to download or upload the whole file after making changes to the file. You will only need to save the part that has been updated (which doesn't consume much memory and time). It will be much easier to save the different versions of the document in various chunks.

We have seen the case of one file, which is divided into various chunks. What if there are multiple files? Then we have to know which chunks belong to which file. To keep information like this, there will be a need to create one more file named as a **metadata file**. This file will contain the indexes of the chunks (chunk names and order information). You will have to mention the hash of the chunks (or some reference) in the metadata file and you will also need to sync this file into the cloud. The metadata file can be downloaded from the cloud anytime and the file can be recreated using various chunks.

## Various components for the complete design of a Dropbox

Let's assume we have a client installed on our computer that can upload files (an app installed on your computer) and this particular client has 4 basic components. These basic components include Watcher, Chunker, Indexer, and Internal DB. The Desktop Client Application has its use in that it monitors the folders that are identified as workspace or sync folders and then synchronizes them with your remote Cloud Storage. The Desktop Client works with the Synchronization Service to operate file metadata updates (e.g. file size, name, date, modification date.). The desktop client also works with the backend Cloud Storage for saving the actual files. The desktop client must meet the following requirements; ability to upload and download files, detecting if there are any changes in files in the sync folder and it also handles any conflict resulting from concurrent updates. .

## Discuss the Client Components

- **Watcher** is the one responsible for monitoring the sync folder for all users' activities such as updating folders, creating folders and deleting folders/files. The watcher also notifies the indexer and the chunker if any action has been performed in the files or folders.
- **Chunker** is the one that helps to break the files into multiple small pieces named chunks and then upload the file to the cloud storage while assigning the file a unique id or hash of these chunks. The chunks can be joined together to recreate the file. If there is any change in the files, the chunking algorithm will detect that specific chunk which is modified and saved to the cloud storage. It reduces synchronization time, band-width usage and storage space in the cloud.
- Indexer will be the one to process the events received from the Watcher and then update the

internal database with details about the chunks of the modified files. Once the chunks have been submitted successfully to the Cloud Storage, the Indexer will then communicate with the Synchronization Service using the Message Queuing Service to update the Metadata Database with the changes.

- Internal Database helps to keep track of the chunks, files, their location in the file system and their versions.

## Metadata Database

The Metadata Database is the one that is responsible for maintaining the versioning and metadata detail about users, files/chunks and workspaces. The Metadata Database can either be a relational database like MySQL, or a NoSQL database. The only thing here is to ensure that the data consistency requirement is met.

Below is a snippet of sample metadata;

```
{"
    chunk_id": "string",
    "chunk_order": "number",
    "object": {"
        version": "number",
        "is_folder": "boolean",
        "modified": "number",
        "file_name": "string",
        "file_extention": "string",
        "file_size": "number",
        "file_path": "string",
        "user": {"
            user_name": "string",
            "email": "string",
            "quota_limit": "number",
            "quota_used": number,
            "device": {"
                device_name": "string"" sync_folder": "string"
            }
        }
    }
}
```


## Message Queuing Service

A critical part of the reference architecture is a messaging system that will be able to handle a decent amount of reads and writes. A scalable Message Queuing Service that enables asynchronous message-based communication between the synchronization service and the clients will fit the application requirement best. This Message Queuing Service will support asynchronous and any loosely coupled message-based communication between distributed parts of the system. The Message Queuing Service will meet the following requirements; must be of high performance, must be highly scalable and must be able to persistently save any number of messages in a highly reliable and available queue. Load balancing coupled with elasticity for multiple instances of the synchronization is provided by the Message Queuing

Service. Two types of queue can be in the message queuing services, which are the Request queue and the Response queue. The Request Queue is a typical global queue that is usually shared among all clients. Any request by a client to update the Metadata Database through the Synchronization Service will always be sent to the Request Queue. The Response Queues that correspond to individual subscribed clients are the ones that are responsible for delivering the update messages to each client. Once the message has been received by a client, the message will be deleted from the queue; hence, there is a recognized need to create a separate response queue to handle message sharing.

## Synchronization Service

The Synchronization Service is the component that helps processes file updates from a particular client and then applies the changes made to other subsc- ribed clients. It also assists in synchronizing clients' local databases with the detail stored in the Metadata Database. This helps to manage the metadata of users as well as synchronizing users' files; this, you would agree is the most important part of your system architecture. Obtaining updates from the Cloud storage or sending files and updates to other users and cloud storage is possible with the aid of communication between the desktop clients and the synchronization service.  If any client is not online for a period, it polls the system for any new updates as soon the client comes online. When an update request is received by the synchronization service, it will quickly check with the metadata database for consistency and then go on with the update. A notification is then sent subsequently to all subscribed devices or users and the file update is reported.

## Cloud Storage

The Cloud Storage, otherwise called the Block server, is the one that helps store the chunks of any files uploaded by a particular user. Clients interact directly with Cloud Storage to send and receive items using the API from the cloud provider. Building and maintaining cloud storage from the scratch is very tedious and time demanding, so it is better to use a readymade cloud service like the Amazon S3 cloud service.

# CHAPTER SIX

## DESIGNING TWITTER

---

Twitter, in recent time, has become one of the biggest microblogging and social networking platforms used by millions of people every day across the world. You might have been checking this social media platform to get your daily updates in times past, but what if an interviewer requests you to give a brief rundown of how to design a microblogging website like Twitter? When you are faced with this kind of question in an interviewer, you need to remember that there is no standard answer for an SDI question like this one. Everything all boils down to what you and your interviewer agree on since he is the one administering the question. This is why you need to request your interviewer to be explicit about what he or she expects you to do. This means that it doesn't really matter what tools you will use in your design, but what does matter is your approach and the analysis of the problem at hand.

In this guide, only the core features of Twitter will be discussed, as no one will expect you to design the whole Twitter all within 45 minutes of your interview.

## Discuss About the Core Features

You can first divide the whole system into several key components and then discuss some important features. If there are some other features that the interviewer will want you to add, he will let you know as the interview unfolds. At the moment, the following features of Twitter are only going to be examined;

- Users should be able to send their tweets within a space of a few seconds.
- Tweet timeline(s) should be easily accessible to the users.
- **Timeline:** The Twitter timeline can be split into three parts;
  - *User timeline:* Users can see their own tweet by visiting their own profiles.
  - *Home timeline:* The home timeline contains tweets from other users, particularly users that the owner of the twitter account is following. This is the tweet user sees when he/she log in to www.twitter.com
  - *Search timeline:* Users can search any keyword or tags and tweets related to that keyword or tags will be shown.
- Follow: All users must be able to follow one another by mere tapping on the **follow button.**

- Users should have the ability to tweet millions of followers within a space of few seconds (5 seconds)

## Naive Solution (Synchronous DB queries)

To design something as big as Twitter, you might need to first dabble into some naïve solutions. This will guide us toward the high level architectural design. You can create a solution for;

1. **Data modelling:** You can deploy a relational database such as MySQL and you can make two tables: a user **table (id, username)** and a **tweet table [id, content, user (primary key of user table)]**. The user table will store information of users, while the tweet table will contain tweet messages by users. Two relations are also important here. One is that users can follow each other, while the other is each feed will have a user owner. So there will be a one-to-many-connection between user and tweet table.
2. **Serve feeds:** You need to assemble all the feeds from all individuals that the user is following and then render them in chronological order.

## High level Design

Twitter is a read-heavy application and it requires a system that will allow users to read any information faster. Although, **Redis** can be useful for this purpose but it cannot be relied on solely because there will be a need to save a copy of user centered information and tweets in the database. Here, you can have three main architectures of Twitter that will consist of three tables; **tweet table, user table** and **followers table.**

- Whenever any user creates a profile on www.twitter.com, the entry will always be stored in the User table.

- The Tweet table will contain a tweet by a user along with the ID of the user. Likewise, the user table will have one to many relationships with the tweet table.

- When any user follows another, it will be stored in the Followers Table, and its Redis will also be cached. The User table will also have **one to many relationships** with the Follower table.

## User Timeline Architecture

- To obtain the User Timeline kindly scroll to the user table, obtain the user_id, match the user_id in the tweet table and then obtain all the tweets. This will equally include retweets, save retweets as tweets with original tweet reference. Once this has been accomplished, the tweet can be sorted by date and time and the information on the user timeline will be prompted.

- The approach described above might fail to work as Twitter is a read heavy-system. Another alternative approach is using the **caching layer.** To use this, try and save the user data you obtained for the user timeline in Redis for conveniences. Likewise, you have to keep saving the tweets in Redis to allow anyone that visits the user timeline an easy access to all the tweetS by the user. It is always faster getting user data from Redis than it is to get it from DB.

## Home Timeline Architecture

The home timeline of a user has all the latest tweets of that user and all the pages that the user is following. The main thing here is that you can easily obtain all the users that a particular user is following, obtain all the latest tweets for each of the followers, merge all of these tweets, sort them by dates and times and then display all the tweets on the home timeline of the user. This approach has few drawbacks in that the search operation will take much time since once the tweet table reaches millions. Let us discuss the solution to the drawback as follow; *Fanout Approach:* Fanout literally denotes spreading the data from one point. Whenever a tweet is done by a user (Followee), do some **preprocessing** and then distribute the data into different users (followers) home timelines. With this, you won't necessarily have to make any database queries. You only have to go to the cache by user_id and view the home timeline data in Redis. You can view this approach with the example below;

- User A has three followers and this user has a user timeline cache. User A tweeted something.
- The tweet will move into the back-end through Load Balancer.
- A Server node will save the tweet in DB/cache
- The Server node will assemble all the users that are following User A from the cache.
- The Server node will then inject this tweet into in-memory timelines of user A's followers (fanout)
- All the followers that are following User A will see the tweet of User A in their timeline. The tweet will always be refreshed and updated anytime a user makes a visit to his/her timeline.

***What about a celebrity with millions of followers? Will the approach above work?***

**Weakness (Edge Case):** What if your interviewer asks the question above? How will you answer him/her?

Normally, if there is a celebrity with millions of followers on Twitter, Twitter can use around 3 to 40 minutes for his tweet to flow to his millions of followers. This means that you will need to update millions of home timelines of users, which is not possible to be produced in a range of capabilities. You can adopt the solution below to work around this;

**Solution: Using Mixed Approach (In-memory+ Synchronous calls):**

- You can precompute the home timeline of follower A (following the celebrity) with everyone except the celebrity's tweet(s)
- For every user maintains the list of celebrities in the cache and also who that user is following. When the tweet from the celebrity arrives, you can obtain the celebrity from the list, extract the tweet from the user timeline of that celebrity and then mix his tweet at runtime with other tweets from his follower (follower A).
- Therefore, when follower A accesses his home timeline, his tweet feed will be merged with the celebrity's tweet at load time. So the celebrity's tweet will now be inserted at runtime.

**Other Optimization:** Do not try to compute the timeline for users that are not active (say for over 20 days).


## Searching

Searching for tweets and tags on Twitter is handled by using **Earlybird** which is actually a real-time reverse index based on Lucene. Early Bird carries out an **inverted full-text indexing** operation. This means that anytime a tweet is shared by a user, it will be treated as a document. The tweet will then be split into words, tags, and #tags, and the words are then indexed. The indexing is carried out at a big table or distributed table. In the distributed table, each word has a reference to every tweet that contains that particular word. Let us say a user searches for the word "politics," then you will scroll through the table to find this word, and you will then figure out every reference to all the tweets in the system, and you will have the result that contains the word "politics."

## THINGS YOU NEED TO KNOW BEFORE YOUR NEXT SDI

- **You need to be familiar with the likely questions the interviewer can ask you during the course of the interview:** Candidates are frequently asked to design a particular system in order to solve a typical open-ended problem. Some of the likely design questions and techniques you can adopt to answer then have been discussed in the previous sections. You should understand that there is no correct answer as everything boils to your ability to think on the spot and provide a plausible way of solving the problem given to you. During SDI, your communication and problem solving skills will be duly evaluated. This is why you must give a step-by-step analysis of how you can tackle the given problem. If any question is not clear, you can ask the interviewer to be explicit about it.

- **Get your hands dirty:** Everyone knows that one panacea to success is adequate preparation. You cannot underestimate the importance of early preparation. It is important to practice with real life scenarios by designing systems on your own prior to the interview day. This allows you to get a good grasp of the concept, and discussing the theoretical part on your interview day will be nothing but a formality. You can visit www.github.com and contribute to open source problems on the platform.
- Set Up a mock interview and practice with your friends.

# About The Author

***Carl Jones*** is a leading behavior research and UX design consultancy specializing in using behavior economics and decision design to drive consumer decision making. He is a behavior design instructor working with over 50 companies to solve their most important behavior challenges.

Carl is also a system expert who had sat, on behalf of recruiters, in many interview panels for System Design. He has insightful opinions about what interviewers need to see and hear. Carl lives in New York with his wife and family.

www.ingramcontent.com/pod-product-compliance
Lightning Source LLC
Chambersburg PA
CBHW071919120726
48001CB00005B/1788